Victorian Seaside Holidays

THE LONDO
www.bro

Mandy Ross

Heinemann
LIBRARY

www.heinemann.co.uk/library
Visit our website to find out more information about **Heinemann Library** books.

To order:

☎ Phone ++44 (0)1865 888066

📄 Send a fax to ++44 (0)1865 314091

💻 Visit the Heinemann Bookshop at *www.heinemann.co.uk/library* to browse our catalogue
and order online.

First published in Great Britain by Heinemann Library, Halley Court, Jordan Hill, Oxford OX2 8EJ, part of Harcourt Education. Heinemann is a registered trademark of Harcourt Education Ltd.

Editorial: Lucy Thunder and Helen Cannons
Design: Ron Kamen and Paul Davies
Picture Research: Rebecca Sodergren and Liz Savery
Production: Edward Moore
Originated by Repro Multi-Warna
Printed and bound in China by South China Printing Company
The paper used to print this book comes from sustainable resources.

10 digit ISBN 0 431 12143 5 (hardback)
13 digit ISBN 978 0 431 12143 7 (hardback)
08 07 06 05 04
10 9 8 7 6 5 4 3 2 1

10 digit ISBN 0 431 12148 6 (paperback)
13 digit ISBN 978 0 431 12148 2 (paperback)
09 08 07
10 9 8 7 6 5 4 3

British Library Cataloguing in Publication Data

Ross, Mandy
Victorian seaside holidays. – (Life in the past)
394.2′6941′09034

A full catalogue record for this book is available from the British Library.

Acknowledgements
The Publishers are grateful to the following for permission to reproduce photographs:
Advertising Archive p**25**; Alamy Images pp**7**, **19**, **23**, **28**; Billie Love Historical Collection p**9**; Bridgeman Art Library p**14**; Corbis/Bettmann p**21**; Corbis/Jon Sparks p**29**; Fine Art Photographic Library/Malletts p**10**; Fine Art Photographic Library/Courtesy of N. R. Omell Gallery, London p**6**; Fine Art Photographic Library/Waterhouse-Dodd p**12**; Hulton Archive pp**4**, **8**, **15**, **16**, **24**, **26**, **27**; Mary Evans Picture Library pp**11**, **13**, **17**, **20**; Robert Opie p**18**; Topham Picturepoint pp**5**, **22**.

Cover photo of the seaside resort of Southsea in the 1890s reproduced with permission of Hulton Archive.

Our thanks to Jane Shuter for her assistance in the preparation of this book.

Every effort has been made to contact copyright holders of any material reproduced in this book. Any omissions will be rectified in subsequent printings if notice is given to the Publishers.

Disclaimer

Contents

Words written in bold, **like this**, are explained in the Glossary.

Queen Victoria **reigned** in Britain from 1837 to 1901. People who lived during this time are called Victorians. Life was very different in 1837. There were no motor cars, aeroplanes or computers then.

☞

Queen Victoria in a horse-drawn carriage.

During Victoria's reign, men, women and children began to work in new factories in towns. They worked long hours, for very little money. At the start of Victoria's reign, only rich people could afford holidays.

This Victorian photograph shows girls working in a cotton mill. ☞

Holidays then and now

Seaside holidays grew very popular during Victoria's **reign**. People thought the air was clean and refreshing beside the sea. They thought bathing in the sea was healthy, too.

☞ Victorian families relaxing and playing on the sand.

Today people still go on seaside holidays. They go for many of the same reasons as the Victorians – for sunshine and fresh air, to play in the sand, and to have a change from home and work.

These children today are making sandcastles on the beach.

All aboard!

By the 1840s, railways were being built right around Britain. People could now travel more quickly and cheaply. Soon many people were travelling by train to the seaside.

 This picture shows a busy Victorian railway station in 1869.

Towards the end of the Victorian age, motor cars were **invented**. Later, motor coaches called **charabancs** became popular. Charabancs took groups of people out for a day's trip, called an **excursion**.

These people have arrived by charabanc at a seaside town in Devon.

Beside the seaside

As the railways spread, holiday **resorts** grew up along the coasts. Most people travelled to the seaside nearest to their home. For example, most Glasgow factory workers went on holiday along the Firth of Clyde.

This painting shows the popular Victorian resort of Scarborough, in north-east England.

Holidaymakers sent postcards home. They told friends and relatives what a good time they were having – just as people do today.

This message is from a Victorian postcard:

Dear Win,
Just a line to let you know we are enjoying ourselves A1,

Love Reg

Rich and poor

Rich people took long holidays. Some families stayed by the sea for several weeks. Many stayed in expensive hotels. Some rich families started to go abroad for their holidays, too.

 Rich people could afford long, luxurious holidays, like these people in France.

Ordinary people also started having short holidays. Many factories closed for a week in the summer. Factory workers saved up to stay in cheaper **lodging houses**.

Coachloads of London children set off for a day's holiday in 1876.

Dressing up, covering up

Victorians liked to keep their bodies private. On the beach, men, women and children wore their normal clothes. Everything must have got very sandy!

 People are fully dressed on the beach.

Everyone wore their best clothes at the seaside. Holidays were a chance to show off fashionable clothes. If they could afford to, people bought new clothes for their holidays.

bowler hat

☞ These people on the **promenade** at Littlehampton, Sussex, are wearing suits and dresses.

A dip in the sea

Victorians thought that bathing in the sea was healthy. Even people who could not swim went in for a dip. They changed into their swimsuits in wooden huts on wheels called **bathing machines**.

Bathing machines were wheeled right into the sea.

bathing machine

At the start of Victoria's **reign**, swimsuits had long sleeves and legs. Even so, men and women swam in different parts of the sea at many **resorts**. By the end of Victorian times, things were less strict.

These bathing suits are from 1876. With their short sleeves and legs, they are quite daring!

On the beach

Victorian children played in the sand with buckets and spades, just as children do today. They were kept busy with other activities, too, such as looking for wildlife in rockpools.

This Victorian poem is about a visit to the beach.

'When I was down beside the sea
A wooden spade they gave to me
To dig the sandy shore.
My holes were empty like a cup,
In every hole the sea came up,
Till it could come no more.'

by Robert Louis Stevenson

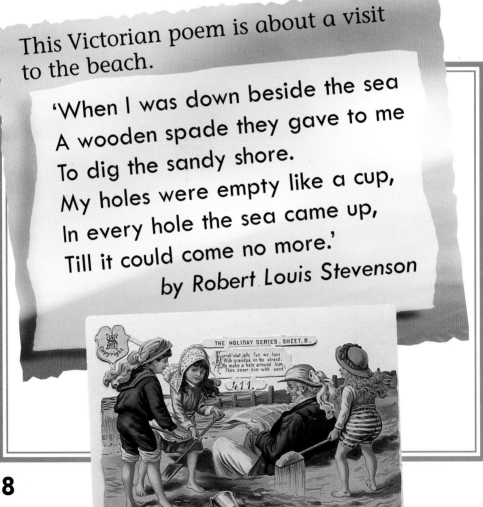

There were children's entertainments on the beach. Puppet shows were very popular. Punch and Judy was a traditional favourite. A donkey ride along the sand was another treat.

Mr Punch

Children watching a Punch and Judy puppet show on the sand.

puppet theatre

Picnics and snacks

Victorian picnics were often quite grand. Rich people's **servants** would pack a basket full of treats. They used proper cups, saucers and plates. There was a lot to carry on to the beach!

☞ People drinking tea on the beach.

All kinds of food and snacks were sold at stalls along the seafront. Seafood was popular, such as **whelks** or jellied eels. Ice cream was an expensive treat.

This picture shows a wooden machine for making ice cream. It was used before electric freezers were **invented**.

TINGLEY'S PATENT
HORIZONTAL
ICE-CREAM FREEZER

Is recommended for FAMILIES, HOTELS, SALOONS, and WHOLESALE MANUF TURERS

As the best Ice-Cream Freezer in the market.

It saves ICE,
Saves TIME,
Saves LABOR,

And produces the finest quality of Cream known to the Art.

Send for Descriptive Catalogue.

CHAS. G. BLATCHLEY, Manufacturer,
506 COMMERCE STREET,
Philadelphia, Pa.

Piers and promenades

There were lots of things to do at the seaside, as well as playing on the beach. Holidaymakers could enjoy strolling along the seafront on new **promenades**. Many **resorts** had a bandstand and beautiful flower gardens.

A band playing on the promenade by the sea at Rhyl, Wales.

bandstand

During Victorian times, attractions were built to make resorts more popular. The Blackpool Tower was a famous attraction. In many resorts a **pier** was built stretching right out over the sea, like a long bridge.

The Blackpool Tower was built between 1892 and 1894. ☞

Trips and treats

Victorian holidaymakers enjoyed **excursions**. Paddleboats and **steamers** sailed along the coast for a short trip to see the sights.

paddle wheel

steam funnel

Taking a ride on the water was very popular.

Every **resort** had a theatre. Holidaymakers could see musical shows, acrobats and other exciting treats. Resorts competed to book the most popular circus, pantomime or performers for the summer season.

A poster advertising a show by a Victorian trapeze artist called Graceful Gertrella.

All the fun of the fair

Funfairs were very popular during Victorian times. There were big dippers, merry-go-rounds and lots of other amusements at the seaside. Many of these rides are still popular today. Have you ever been to a funfair?

A merry-go-round at a Victorian fairground.

Victorians loved to see strange and wonderful shows. They paid to watch people do tricks at the fairground, such as weight-lifting or dancing on horseback. Animal acts were very popular.

This Victorian strongman is lifting heavy weights, called dumb-bells.

Let's find out!

Have you ever been to the seaside in Britain? Many Victorian seaside **resorts** are popular today. You can still see grand Victorian hotels, **piers** and other buildings there.

These children are enjoying donkey rides on Blackpool beach. The tower is in the background.

Today many people fly abroad for holidays in warmer places. Some resorts are less popular now, and they are growing shabby. Do you think we should have more seaside holidays in Britain?

In the winter, very few people go to seaside resorts. The piers are not as well looked after as they used to be.

Timeline

1830 First passenger steam trains run between Liverpool and Manchester

1837 Victoria is crowned Queen of Great Britain

1841 Thomas Cook organizes his first railway **excursion** from Leicester to Loughborough

1843 Wooden machine for making ice cream is **invented**

1845 Osborne House, on the Isle of Wight, becomes Queen Victoria's seaside home

1851 The Great Exhibition is held at the Crystal Palace, London. Ice cream-making machines are among the items on display.

1854 British troops fight in the Crimean War against Russia

1861 Prince Albert, Victoria's husband, dies

1871 Government passes laws allowing **bank holidays**

1880 First electric trams and trains come into use

1885 Motor car is invented in Germany

1895 Blackpool Tower is opened. It copied the Eiffel Tower in Paris.

1901 Queen Victoria dies at Osborne House

Glossary

bank holiday day when banks and other offices closed for workers' holidays

bathing machine small wooden hut on wheels for changing in. Bathing machines were wheeled into the sea so that bathers could get straight into the water.

charabanc early coach. The name in French means 'wagon with benches'. At first they were pulled by horses, but later had motors.

excursion short journey taken for pleasure

invent to make something in a new way, or find a new way of doing something

lodging house home with rooms to rent to holidaymakers

pier platform built for walking out over the sea, made of metal and wood

promenade paved road built along the seafront

reign to rule as a king or queen, or the period of time a ruler spends on the throne

resort place where people go on holiday

servant someone who is paid to work in somebody else's house, doing cooking or cleaning

steamer steam ship

whelk type of shellfish that can be eaten

Find out more

More books to read

A Victorian Child goes to the Seaside, Christine Butterwort (Heinemann Primary, 2002)

Sport and Leisure in Victorian Times, Neil Morris (Belitha Press, 2000)

Places and websites to visit

www.nationaltrust.org.uk
The National Trust has information about historic buildings to visit in your area.

www.museumofchildhood.org.uk
The Museum of Childhood, London has displays about many aspects of Victorian childhood.

Index